Barack Obama

History Maker Bios

Jane Sutcliffe

BARNES & NOBLE

NEW YORK

For the students of Somers Elementary School,
because this was your idea.

Text © 2010 by Jane Sutcliffe
Illustrations © 2010 by Lerner Publishing Group, Inc.

This 2010 edition published by Barnes & Noble, Inc.
by arrangement with Lerner Publications Company, a division of
Lerner Publishing Group, Inc., Minneapolis, MN.

Illustrations by Tad Butler

ISBN-13: 978-1-4351-1897-3

Printed and bound in the United States of America

1 3 5 7 9 10 8 6 4 2

The quotes in this book have been drawn from many sources, and are assumed to be accurate as quoted
in their previously published forms. Although every effort has been made to verify the quotes and sources,
the publishers cannot guarantee their perfect accuracy.

All Web sites and URLs in this book are current at the point of publication. However, Web sites may be
taken down and URLs may change after publication without notice. The Publisher and the Author are
not responsible for the content contained in any specific Web site featured in this book, nor shall they be
liable for any loss or damage arising from the information contained in this book.

TABLE OF CONTENTS

INTRODUCTION

When Barack Obama was a boy, he posed for his class picture. There he was, smiling along with his classmates. His was the only black face in the class. Hardly anyone would have pointed to him and said, "*He's* going to be president one day." For one thing, Barack came from an unusual background. He had a strange name. But most of all, the United States had never had an African American president.

In the end, none of that mattered. Barack Obama made history. He became the first black president of the United States. Americans could proudly point to him and say, "He is our forty-fourth president."

This is his story.

1 "CALL ME BARRY"

Barack Obama was born on August 4, 1961, in Honolulu, Hawaii. But his story really began earlier, with his parents.

Barack's parents could not have seemed more different from each other. His mother, Ann Dunham, was white. She had been born in Kansas. His father, Barack Hussein Obama, was black. He was from Kenya, a country in Africa.

Ann and Barack met at the University of Hawaii. They fell in love. In the 1960s, marriage between a black person and a white person was very unusual. They got married anyway. The next year, Barack Hussein Obama Jr. was born. His nickname was Barry.

When Barry was two years old, his father had a chance to study at Harvard University in Massachusetts. He left his wife and son behind. The separation led to divorce. Barry and his mother moved in with her parents, Stanley and Madelyn Dunham. Barry called them Gramps and Toot. (That was short for *Tutu*, the Hawaiian word for "grandparent.")

Barry (RIGHT) spends time with his mother, Ann, in Hawaii.

A few years later, Ann married again. Her new husband, Lolo, was from the country of Indonesia, in Southeast Asia. When Barry was six, he, his mother, and Lolo moved to Indonesia.

For Barry, Indonesia was a grand adventure. In the backyard, he found a pond with real baby crocodiles. He had a pet ape named Tata. He spent his days catching crickets and flying kites.

But there was a sad side to the country too. Many people were very poor. Beggars often came to the door. Some were children. Many of them were sick.

Barry (RIGHT) sits with Lolo, Ann, and Barry's sister Maya in Indonesia. Later, Ann and Lolo divorced.

Ann worried about Barry's education in such a poor country. Every morning, she woke him before dawn. She taught Barry herself before he left for school. Before long, though, they had finished all the lessons. Barry was nine years old. It was time for him to go to an American school.

At the airport, Barry said good-bye to his mother, stepfather, and new baby sister, Maya. In Hawaii, he said hello again to Gramps and Toot. Barry lived with them while he went to school. Barry attended Punahou Academy in Honolulu. He was one of only a few black students there.

Barry (BACK ROW, THIRD FROM LEFT) smiles for his fifth-grade class picture.

One day, he came home from school to find a stranger in his grandparents' apartment. His father had come from Africa to visit. He brought Barry some wooden carvings. Barack and Barry danced to African music together. But sometimes his father was bossy. When Barry wanted to watch TV, Barack told him to go study. After a tense month, Barack left.

The only black relative Barry knew was gone again. Barry had begun to see that being black in the United States meant something—but he wasn't exactly sure what.

When Barry was ten years old, his father visited him in Hawaii.

He knew that sometimes people treated him differently because of his skin color. A girl at school wanted to touch his wiry hair. A boy asked if his father ate people.

Once, he got on the elevator at his grandparents' apartment building. A white woman had gotten on ahead of him. The woman complained that Barry was following her. She refused to apologize even after she learned that Barry lived there.

When Barry looked in the mirror, he saw a young black man. But he didn't know how to be black. And no one was there to teach him.

He decided to act like the black characters he saw on TV. He started acting tough. He cursed. Was that what it meant to be black?

As he got older, he started smoking and drinking. He tried drugs. Was that what it meant to be black?

Barry's grandparents congratulate him at his high school graduation.

Barry's grades began to slip. Still, he was a bright student. In June 1979, he graduated from high school. He planned to attend Occidental College in Los Angeles, California, the following year.

A few days before he left Hawaii, someone asked him what he expected to get out of college. Barry had to admit he didn't know.

2 BARACK

In the fall of 1979, Barry left Hawaii behind and moved to Los Angeles. He became a student at Occidental. But he still had the same questions about who he was.

This building is on the campus of Occidental College.

Most of his friends in college were African American. Barry still thought he had to act a certain way to fit in. Once he said a mean thing about another black student. He accused him of trying too hard to be liked by white people. One of Barry's friends corrected him. Don't be so quick to judge how other folks are supposed to act, he told Barry.

Little by little, Barry learned what was important to his friends. Don't judge others. Clean up your own messes. Think of other people, not just yourself. Those were the same lessons he'd learned from his white mother and grandparents. They weren't so different after all.

Students like Barry held rallies on college campuses.

Barry saw there were places in the world where black people had few rights. One was the country of South Africa. He thought it was wrong that Occidental had invested money with South African businesses. He began speaking out. He wrote letters to college officials. He helped set up rallies. He noticed that other students listened to his opinions. For the first time, he found that his words could change people's minds.

In 1981, Barry decided to move to New York City.

After two years, Barry switched to a bigger college in New York City. He entered Columbia University. He was twenty years old. But to the other students, he seemed older. Barry had grown into a thoughtful and serious-minded young man. He began calling himself Barack. He spent most of his time on his schoolwork.

His hard work paid off. In 1983, Barack graduated from Columbia. At first, he found an office job in New York. But that wasn't what he wanted to do.

A Sad Call, a Lost Chance

Barack had planned to travel to Africa to visit his father after college. Then one day, he got a phone call. It was from an aunt in Kenya. His father had died in a car accident. He would never have a chance to see his father again.

He decided he wanted to be a community organizer—even though he wasn't quite sure what that was. All he knew was that he saw a world in need of change. And he wanted to help change it.

Before long, Barack found himself with a new home and a new job. His new home was Chicago, Illinois. His job was helping people in poor neighborhoods in the city. There were plenty of problems in the neighborhoods. But Barack wasn't supposed to solve the problems himself. His job was to show people how to work together to bring about change.

Children walk through the Altgeld Gardens neighborhood. Barack worked hard to improve things for the people who lived there.

Much of Barack's work was in a neighborhood called Altgeld Gardens. The "gardens" part of the name was a bit of a joke. Altgeld sat smack between a dump and a waste plant. A filthy river ran nearby. The buildings were run-down and smelly. The people who lived there were poor, black, and ignored by most city officials.

Barack helped people work to improve things at Altgeld. He planned meetings and rallies. He set up a bus trip to meet with public officials.

There were some successes. City workers fixed streets and cleaned up playgrounds. Residents convinced officials to bring jobs into the neighborhood. The people in Altgeld fought to have city workers test their homes for asbestos, a material that can cause cancer.

But mostly, the successes were small. One resident told Barack, "Ain't nothing gonna change, Mr. Obama."

Barack saw that real change would have to come from new laws. And lawmakers made laws. To get things done, he would have to become a lawmaker. To do that, he decided, he would go to law school.

But first, he would take a trip he'd been meaning to take for a very long time. He would go to Kenya to meet his African family.

3 A RISING STAR

"**A**h, Barry . . . we may not have much in Kenya—but so long as you are here, you will always have something to eat!" For weeks, Barack visited his family in Kenya. He met brothers, sisters, aunts, uncles, and cousins. They talked and laughed during long family dinners.

Barack (LEFT) sits with Grandmother Sarah; his sister, Auma Obama; and his stepmother, Kezia Obama.

In a little village, at the foot of a mango tree, he found his father's grave. He cried for the man he barely knew. Then, too soon, it was time for good-byes. It was time for Barack to start law school.

Harvard University in Cambridge, Massachusetts, has one of the best law schools in the country. There, Barack spent long hours studying. By the end of his first year, he was one of the top students.

Most of the law students had strong opinions. They liked to talk and argue. And they all thought their point of view was the right one—the *only* right one. Barack was different. He listened to everyone's ideas. Then he tried to get people to agree. That earned him the respect of even the most hotheaded students. In 1989, the law students chose him to be president of the law school's publication, the *Harvard Law Review*.

No African American student had ever received that honor. Suddenly, Barack was big news. His picture was in newspapers. A publisher wanted him to write about his life.

Barack holds a copy of the HARVARD LAW REVIEW.

All this meant that Barack had to work even harder! Of course, he didn't spend all his time thinking about schoolwork. He had met smart, beautiful Michelle Robinson. Michelle had already graduated from Harvard Law School. The two found they had many things in common. They even laughed at the same things. Soon Barack was in love.

In 1991, Barack graduated from law school. He had not forgotten about being a lawmaker. He went back to Chicago. On October 3, 1992, he and Michelle were married there.

THE FUTURE MRS. OBAMA

Barack met Michelle at a law firm in Chicago. He was a law student working at a summer job. She was his supervisor. At first, Michelle didn't want to date someone she was supposed to be in charge of. But Barack soon won her over.

Students enjoyed Barack's law school classes.

Barack took a job as a lawyer. He also taught law courses at the University of Chicago. His first book, *Dreams from My Father,* was published in 1995. Then an opportunity arose. A state senator announced that she was stepping down from her job. Her decision gave Barack his big chance. He decided to run for her job in the state senate.

Running for office means meeting as many voters as possible. Barack knocked on doors and rang doorbells. He spoke at church socials and went to beauty parlors and barbershops. "If two guys were standing on a corner," he said, "I would cross the street to hand them campaign literature."

Most people wanted to know where he got his funny name. But they must have remembered that name. In November 1996, Barack Obama won the election. At last, as he had planned, he was a lawmaker. He was thirty-five years old.

Barack worked hard to make new laws. He was especially interested in laws that helped poor people and protected their rights. Other lawmakers sometimes disagreed with Barack's ideas. Just as he had in law school, Barack listened to their opinions. Then he tried to find a way to get both sides to agree. That not only earned him respect. It helped him pass good laws.

The state senate meets at the capitol in Springfield, Illinois.

Barack worked hard as an Illinois state senator.

By 1998, Barack had become a respected state senator. And there was more happy news. He and Michelle had a baby daughter, born on July 4. They named her Malia.

Still, Barack was restless. All those good laws helped only the people of Illinois. He wanted to do the same thing for the whole country. He made a big decision. He would run for the U.S. Congress.

This race would not be so easy. No one was stepping down this time. The African American man who held the job was well known and well liked.

This time, when Barack knocked on doors, people weren't so happy to see him. Black voters wondered why Barack was trying to beat someone who was already helping them. By Election Day, Barack knew he was going to lose. He did—badly.

The whole thing had been a mistake. Barack had to face a hard possibility. Maybe his career wasn't going to work out as he'd planned.

Barack makes a speech after losing the race for U.S. Congress. Michelle and Malia are at his side.

4 THE SPEECH

Barack went back to his job as a state senator. But after his loss in the election, he began to wonder. When people saw him, did the word *loser* flash through their minds?

Barack worked hard making speeches and meeting voters. His work often kept him away from home. In 2001, his second daughter, Natasha, was born. Barack and Michelle nicknamed her Sasha. Barack had two little girls who needed him at home. He began to think about quitting politics altogether.

That wouldn't be easy for Barack. He
liked what he was doing. He liked the thrill
of the crowds. He liked shaking hands and
talking to people. And by 2002, he had
a lot to talk about. President George W.
Bush was threatening to go to war with
the country of Iraq. He claimed that the
head of the country was hiding dangerous
weapons. The weapons had to be found
and destroyed.
The only way
to do that, the
president said,
was to invade
the country.

In 2002, President
George W. Bush
(SEATED) signed a
law that would let
the United States
invade Iraq.

Some people held rallies against invading Iraq.

Many people and politicians agreed. They wanted the president to keep them safe, no matter what. Other people said no. No one had found any secret weapons in Iraq. And Iraq had not attacked the United States.

What did Barack think? He spoke at a rally against the war. Many people there were wearing buttons saying "War Is Not an Option." The button wearers were expecting to hear Barack speak out against all war. But he didn't. He knew that some wars were worth fighting. He told the crowd, "I am not opposed to all wars. I'm opposed to dumb wars." And the war with Iraq, he said, was a dumb war. Such a war might last years and cost thousands of American lives.

Barack's speech earned him a lot of attention. He still wanted to help make laws for people throughout the country. He decided to run for the U.S. Senate. But a number of other people had the same idea. And most of them were better known in the state of Illinois than Barack. He would have to work hard to stand out.

Barack crisscrossed the state. He met people in cities, in small towns, and on farms. In churches and around kitchen tables, he listened to their problems. They knew that government couldn't solve all their problems. But it should at least help, they told him.

Barack greets people in Springfield, Illinois.

Black voters had always liked Barack. Many people were surprised to see how well he connected with white voters too. But for Barack, speaking with white voters was just like talking with his grandparents.

Once, he gave a speech alongside John Kerry. Kerry was running for U.S. president. He immediately liked Barack's easy style of speaking. Kerry asked Barack to give an important speech. Barack would give it at a large meeting, the Democratic National Convention, on July 27, 2004. Thousands of people would be there to watch. Millions more would see him on TV.

NICE TO MEET YOU, MR. ALABAMA

In his speeches, Barack often poked fun at his odd name. People were always getting it wrong, he said. Sometimes they called him "Alabama" or "Yo' Mama."

The Democratic National Convention gave Barack the chance to be seen and heard around the world.

Most of the politicians at the convention were well known. But few people had ever heard of Barack Obama. So Barack told them his story. He told them about his father from Kenya and his mother from Kansas. He told them about the hopes they had had for their son.

Other politicians focused on what divided Americans. Barack talked about what they all shared—the same hopes and dreams his parents and grandparents had had. He said that in America, there's "a belief that we're all connected as one people. . . . There's not a black America and white America and Latino America and Asian America—there's the United States of America."

When he was finished, people clapped and cheered. Some had tears in their eyes. Barack was no longer an unknown.

Of course, he wasn't a U.S. senator yet either. He still had an election to win. But suddenly, Barack was a star. Wherever he spoke, huge crowds turned out. Everyone wanted to shake his hand. So it was really no surprise when he won the Illinois election to the U.S. Senate.

Barack marches in a parade during his campaign for the U.S. Senate.

Vice President Dick Cheney (RIGHT) poses with the Obamas as Barack becomes a U.S. senator.

In January 2005, Barack officially became a U.S. senator. After the ceremony, he and his family walked outside. Six-year-old Malia turned to her father. "Daddy, are you going to be president?" she asked.

It was a question a lot of people were asking.

5 "A POLITICS OF HOPE"

A spotlight seemed to be shining on the new senator. After his big speech, people all over the country wanted to hear him speak. Television reporters wanted to interview him. Over and over, he heard the same question. Would he run for president? He kept saying no.

Barack just wanted to think about his new job. He was used to worrying about the problems of one state. Trying to solve the problems of a country was a much bigger task. He knew he had a lot to learn.

In 2006, Barack's second book was published. He wrote about the same ideas he'd spoken about in his convention speech. For too long, he wrote, politicians had tried to divide people into this group or that. But politics should not divide people. It should build on the hopes that pull people together. In his speech, he'd called his idea "a politics of hope." He called his book *The Audacity of Hope.* (*Audacity* means "courage or daring.")

Barack greets people at a book signing.

Tim Russert (RIGHT) talks to Barack about his new book on the show MEET THE PRESS.

Barack traveled around the country talking about his book. His views made sense to many people. They liked the idea of a new kind of politics. They liked this bright young man with the calm voice.

People had never stopped asking if Barack would run for president. Finally, Barack stopped saying no. He said yes. But he couldn't win just because of one speech and a couple of books. Many people said he didn't have enough experience to be president. After all, he had only been a U.S. senator for two years.

"I know I haven't spent a lot of time learning the ways of Washington," he answered. "But I've been there long enough to know that the ways of Washington must change." And change was just what many people wanted. They were unhappy with the way President Bush was running the country. Families did not have money to pay for the health care they needed. Workers were losing their jobs.

In Iraq, the war dragged on and on. Thousands of soldiers had been killed. And none of the feared weapons were ever found in Iraq. Of all the major candidates running for president, only Barack had spoken out against the war. The crowds grew.

U.S. soldiers take cover behind a wall in Iraq.

Barack speaks at the Democratic National Convention.

But some people said that Americans weren't ready for *that* much change. Sure Barack was a nice fellow, they said. But white voters would never vote for a black president. Other angry voices were raised. Barack's former pastor called the country a failure. God would damn the United States for mistreating its black citizens, he said.

Barack decided it was time to speak to Americans about race. The country's history of slavery had left the nation in pain, he said. Black people and white people were too often angry with one another. All people were going to have to work together to solve the country's problems. Only in that way could Americans make a more perfect United States.

*Michelle and Barack (LEFT) and Jill and Joe Biden
(RIGHT) greet the crowd. Joe Biden was chosen to be the
candidate for vice president.*

At last, the Democratic Party chose
Barack to be their candidate for president.
The Republican Party chose John McCain.
The two candidates made speeches. They
debated each other.

Finally, on November 4, 2008, voters made
their choice. By evening, the news came.
The votes had been counted. Barack had
made history. He would be the first African
American president of the United States.

Barack and his family wave to a cheering crowd. Barack gave a victory speech on the night he won the election.

Across the United States, people cheered. Some cried or screamed for joy. People around the world shared the excitement. Barack, the president-elect, spoke to a huge crowd in Chicago. People around the world watched on television. "If there is anyone out there who still doubts that America is a place where all things are possible... , " he told them, "tonight is your answer."

OOPS, MR. PRESIDENT!

Barack actually took the oath of office twice. He was supposed to repeat the words of the oath after the chief justice of the United States. But Chief Justice John Roberts flubbed some of the words. He and Barack repeated the whole thing again the next day—just to be sure.

On January 20, 2009, Barack raised his right hand. He took the oath of office of the president of the United States. He promised to "preserve, protect, and defend the Constitution of the United States." It was the beginning of a new chapter in Barack Obama's story. And it was the beginning of a new chapter in the history of the United States.

TIMELINE

In the year . . .

1967   he moved to Indonesia with his mother and stepfather.

1971   he returned to Hawaii to live with his grandparents.   Age 9

1979   he graduated from Punahou Academy in June.

he entered Occidental College in August.

1981   he transferred to Columbia University.

1983   he graduated from Columbia University.

1985   he began work as a community organizer in Chicago, Illinois.

1990   he became the first African American president of the *Harvard Law Review*.   Age 28

1991   he graduated from Harvard Law School.

1992   he married Michelle Obama.

1995   his first book, *Dreams from My Father*, was published.

1996   he became an Illinois state senator.

1998   his daughter Malia was born.

2001   his daughter Natasha (Sasha) was born.

2004   he delivered a speech at the Democratic National Convention in July.   Age 42

he was elected to the U.S. Senate in November.

2005   he officially became a U.S. senator in January.

2006   his second book, *The Audacity of Hope*, was published.

2009   he became the forty-fourth president of the United States.   Age 47

WATCHING HISTORY HAPPEN

Almost two million people gathered in Washington, D.C., to watch Barack become president. A sea of faces stretched as far as the eye could see.

Some of those faces belonged to young people. Some children came with families. Some came with teachers on class trips. Many were African Americans. They had heard parents or grandparents speak of the hurts they had suffered. They came with hope for change. "Many of my ancestors have been waiting for this change," one young woman said, "and I'm glad that I can be part of it."

And who knows? Maybe someday, one of those children will stand where Barack stood that day. Maybe one of those faces in the crowd belongs to someone who will one day become president, just like Barack Obama.

Further Reading

Brill, Marlene Targ. *Barack Obama: President for a New Era.* **Minneapolis: Lerner Publications Company, 2009.** This is a detailed look at Barack's life, from his youth through his inauguration in 2009.

Brill, Marlene Targ. *Michelle Obama: From Chicago's South Side to the White House.* **Minneapolis: Lerner Publications Company, 2009.** This biography of Michelle tells about her childhood, her law career, and her thoughts on being First Lady.

Grimes, Nikki, and Bryan Collie. *Barack Obama: Son of Promise, Child of Hope.* **New York: Simon & Schuster, 2008.** This is a picture book story within a story told by a mother to her young African American son.

Obama, Barack. *Yes, We Can! A Salute to Children from President Obama's Victory Speech.* **New York: Orchard Books, 2009.** This book is a message to the country's children from Barack Obama.

Websites

Barack Obama Speech at 2004 DNC Convention
http://www.youtube.com/watch?v=eWynt87PaJ0 Watch the moving speech that introduced a nation to Barack Obama.

The Briefing Room—the Blog
http://www.whitehouse.gov/blog/ Keep up with what President Obama is doing by checking out the official White House blog.

SELECT BIBLIOGRAPHY

Finnegan, William. "The Candidate: How the Son of a Kenyan Economist Became an Illinois Everyman." *New Yorker*, May 31, 2004.

Hartford (CT) Courant. "Students Trying to Be Part of History," January 18, 2009, H21.

Mendell, David. *Obama: From Promise to Power.* New York: HarperCollins, 2007.

Obama, Barack. *The Audacity of Hope.* New York: Vintage Books, 2006.

Obama, Barack. "Barack Obama's Remarks at the Democratic Convention." *USA Today*, July 27, 2004. http://www.usatoday.com/news/politicselections/nation/president/2004-07-27-obama-speech-text_x.htm (January 20, 2009).

Obama, Barack. *Dreams from My Father: A Story of Race and Inheritance.* New York: Three Rivers Press, 2004.

Obama, Barack. "Remarks of Illinois State Sen. Barack Obama Against Going to War with Iraq." Organizing for America. October 2, 2002. http://www.barackobama.com/2002/10/02/remarks_of_illinois_state_sen.php (March 24, 2009).

Obama, Barack. "Transcript: Barack Obama's Speech on Race." National Public Radio. March 18, 2008. http://www.npr.org/templates/story/story.php?storyId=88478467 (April 1, 2009).

Obama, Barack. "Transcript of Barack Obama's Speech." CBS News. February 10, 2007. http://www.cbsnews.com/stories/2007/02/10/politics/main2458099.shtml (March 26, 2009).

INDEX

Acknowledgments

For photographs and artwork: The images in this book are used with the permission of: © Jonathan Ferrey/Getty Images, p. 4; AP Photo/Obama Presidential Campaign, pp. 7, 8, 12, 16, 22; Punahou School Archives, p. 9; AP Photo/Obama for America, pp. 10, 24; Occidental College Archives, p. 14; AP Photo/Grecco, p. 15; AP Photo/Charles Rex Arbogast, p. 18; INS News Agency Ltd./Rex Features USA, p. 21; AP Photo/Seth Perlman, pp. 25, 26, 31; AP Photo/ Frank Polich, p. 27; AP Photo/Ron Edmonds, pp. 29, 41; © Erik S. Lesser/Getty Images, p. 30; AP Photo/Charlie Neibergall, pp. 33, 40; © Scott Olson/Getty Images, p. 34; © Alex Wong/Getty Images, pp. 35, 45; AP Photo/Jim Cole, p. 37; © Alex Wong/Getty Images for Meet the Press, p. 38; © David Furst/AFP/Getty Images, p. 39; © Jewel Samad/AFP/Getty Images, p. 42; AP Photo/Jae C. Hong, p. 43. Front cover: © Pete Souza/Obama Transition Office via Getty Images.

For quoted material: p. 6, David Mendell, *Obama: From Promise to Power* (New York: Vintage Books, 2006); pp. 19, 20, Barack Obama, *Dreams from My Father: A Story of Race and Inheritance* (New York: Three Rivers Press, 2004); p. 24, Barack Obama, *The Audacity of Hope* (New York: Vintage Books, 2006); p. 30, Barack Obama, "Remarks of Illinois State Sen. Barack Obama Against Going to War with Iraq" (October 2, 2002); p. 32, William Finnegan, "The Candidate: How the Son of a Kenyan Economist Became an Illinois Everyman" (*New Yorker*, May 31, 2004); pp. 33, 36, Barack Obama, "Barack Obama's Remarks at the Democratic Convention" (*USA Today*, July 27, 2004); p. 39, Barack Obama, "Transcript of Barack Obama's Speech, Springfield, Ill." (CBS News, February 10, 2007); p. 42, Barack Obama, "Transcript of Barack Obama's Victory Speech" (National Public Radio, November 5, 2008); p. 45, *Hartford (CT) Courant*, "Students Trying to Be Part of History" (January 18, 2009, H21).